ARTHRITIS

ARTHRITIS

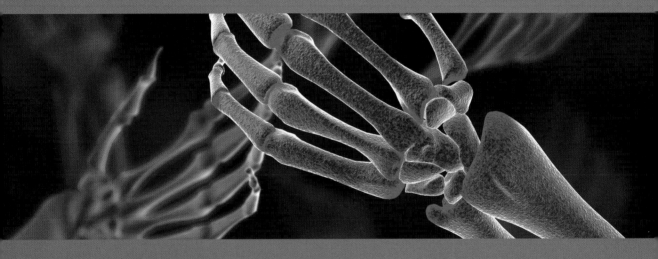

Ruth Bjorklund

Marshall Cavendish
Benchmark
New York

For Olive Edith Gallant

Marshall Cavendish Benchmark
99 White Plains Road
Tarrytown, New York 10591-5502
www.marshallcavendish.us

This book is not intended for use as a substitute for advice, consultation, or treatment by a licensed medical practitioner. The reader is advised that no action of a medical nature should be taken without consultation with a licensed medical practitioner, including action that may seem to be indicated by the contents of this work, since individual circumstances vary and medical standards, knowledge, and practices change with time. The publisher, author, and medical consultants disclaim all liability and cannot be held responsible for any problems that may arise from the use of this book.

Library of Congress Cataloging-in-Publication Data

Bjorklund, Ruth.
Arthritis / by Ruth Bjorklund.
p. cm. — (Health alert)
Summary: "Provides comprehensive information on the causes, treatment, and history of arthritis"—Provided by the publisher.
ISBN 978-0-7614-3984-4
1. Arthritis—Juvenile literature. I. Title.
RC933.B526 2010
616.7'22—dc22

2008051242

Front Cover: X-ray of hand showing rheumatoid arthritis
Title page: X-ray of the knees showing an early stage of osteoarthritis

Photo research by Candlepants Incorporated

Cover Photo: ISM / PhotoTakeUSA.com

The photographs in this book are used by permission and through the courtesy of:

Photo Researchers Inc.: David Mack, 3; Eye of Science, 22; TH Foto-Werbung, 31. *Alamy Images*: Digital Vision, 8; Galina Barskaya, 10; Phototake Inc., 15; Mary Evans Picture Library, 35; Blend Images, 43; Eye-Stock, 46. *PhotoTakeUSA.com*: ISM, 5, 13, 21, 26; Nucleus Medical Art, Inc, 24. *Getty Images*: 3D4Medical.com, 16, 18; Dorling Kindersley, 17; Mason Morfit, 28; Time & Life Pictures, 33; WireImage, 39; Chris Clinton, 41; Barry Yee, 45; Laurence Monneret, 50; Peter Poulides, 53. *Corbis*: Krista Kennell/ZUMA, 36; Flynn Larsen/zefa, 48. *Shutterstock*: 49.

Editor: Joy Bean
Publisher: Michelle Bisson
Art Director: Anahid Hamparian

Printed in Malaysia
6 5 4 3 2 1

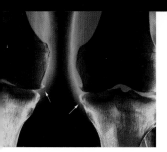

CONTENTS

1

DANIEL'S STORY

Daniel's family loved to ski. They lived near the mountains and skied all winter long. By the time he was ten, Daniel could ski faster backward than his father could ski forward. Sometimes, after a long weekend of skiing, Daniel complained that his wrists and knees hurt. When he told his parents and his doctor, they told him that he had "growing pains."

One day, after a particularly bumpy downhill run, Daniel met up with his parents at the lodge and complained that he felt hot and that his knees really ached. His parents thought he was coming down with the flu and said that a good night's rest was what he needed. Daniel was stiff and achy again in the morning and for several mornings afterward. The family visited the doctor, who agreed that it was the flu and sent Daniel home to rest.

The fever went away, but the pain in Daniel's joints did not. He started taking an over-the-counter pain reliever almost every day, but the pain kept spreading—to his back, ankles, wrists, fingers, and thumbs. He felt stiff in the morning and tired all the time, and he definitely did not feel like skiing. His doctor listened as Daniel described his aches and pains. The doctor said Daniel probably had pulled some muscles or **tendons** while skiing, and he should sit out the rest of the season.

Daniel lived with the aches in his knees, wrists, and back for nearly a year. Though he looked forward to a new ski season, he was worried that he might not be able to keep up with his friends and parents. He visited a new doctor, who performed a few extra tests and asked Daniel a lot of questions. She suggested that Daniel see a specialist called a **rheumatologist**. The rheumatologist confirmed what the new doctor suspected: Daniel had **juvenile rheumatoid arthritis (JRA)**. He and his parents were shocked and confused. They had always thought that arthritis was a disease for old people. But no, they were told, it can happen to anyone at any age. Daniel said, "We were all upset, but we were also happy to have an answer to why I had been in so much pain for so long." After the **diagnosis**, Daniel's life took some new turns. Doctors determined that he had **polyarticular** juvenile rheumatoid arthritis. In this form of the disease, five or more of a person's joints are affected. "Twenty-eight joints, actually," said Daniel.

Daniel soon had to see a whole new group of doctors and therapists. The doctors prescribed medicines that helped ease the pain. The drugs also helped lessen the **inflammation** in his swollen joints. The doctors hoped to keep Daniel's joints protected so that the arthritis would not interfere with his growing body.

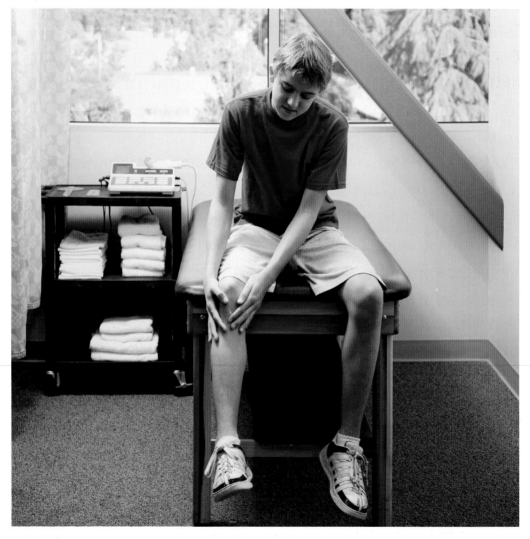

Arthritis can strike at any age. An examination by a doctor will determine whether a person has arthritis or not.

Since his diagnosis, Daniel has continued to take many different medicines, some to reduce inflammation and some to relieve pain. He also takes medicines to counteract the other drugs' nastier side effects, such as nausea, intestinal upset, and vitamin deficiencies. Every few weeks Daniel gets an injection of a very strong drug, methotrexate. The shot makes him feel pretty bad, but the powerful medicine is meant to protect his joints from further damage.

Daniel is grateful for his team of health care providers. "They are amazing," he says. "Without them, I would probably be in a wheelchair by now!" Daniel has always been an active person, and he appreciates how his therapists work with him to keep his body strong. They provide him with exercises specially designed to strengthen his muscles and to keep his joints flexible. And Daniel has no intention of giving up his skis: "I don't plan on stopping skiing until I absolutely can't do it anymore, which hopefully won't happen for a long time!"

Some days, Daniel has to take it easy. He has great friends who come to his house after school to keep him company. "At first," says Daniel, "I didn't know what to tell my friends. I didn't want people to know [about my arthritis] because of what they might think of me or that they might feel bad for me. But as people found out I realized that there was a need for awareness, and I am proud and happy to talk about it to anyone who will listen."

People with arthritis can still enjoy physical activity, as long as they take care to keep their bodies strong.

Daniel has plenty to say to anyone who has been diagnosed with arthritis. "Just keep a positive attitude and you can beat it. I refuse to let it take skiing from me. I guess I just look at it as a challenge to overcome—a challenge that will make me stronger."

2

WHAT IS ARTHRITIS?

Arthritis is a general term for numerous conditions that affect bone joints. Scientists do not know exactly what causes arthritis. Some think the disease is genetic—something that is inherited from your parents. Others think arthritis is caused by infection, **obesity**, bone damage, or another disease. Regardless of the cause or type of arthritis, people with arthritis experience **chronic** pain and swelling in their joints.

More than 46 million people in the United States—and about 300 million people worldwide—suffer from arthritis. Many people think arthritis is a disease that older people get as their joints wear down. It is true that the most common form of arthritis, **osteoarthritis** (AH-stee-oh-ar-THRY-tis), mostly affects people aged sixty and older. But people of any age can develop arthritis. In fact, more than 250,000 children in the United States have one of several forms of the disease. Together these forms are called juvenile arthritis. Some young

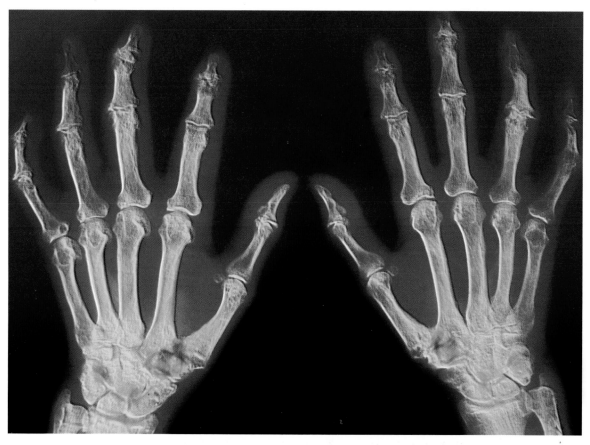

This X-ray shows hands with osteoarthritis, the most common form of arthritis.

people develop osteoarthritis, but the most common form of juvenile arthritis is JRA—the disease that Daniel has.

There are two main types of arthritis—osteoarthritis and rheumatoid arthritis. They are quite different from each other. Osteoarthritis is a condition that occurs when **cartilage** that covers the ends of bones in the joints breaks down and wears away. Rheumatoid arthritis is a disease caused by problems with the body's immune system. To better understand the differences between the two forms of the disease, it helps to be familiar with the systems in the body that are most involved: the **musculoskeletal system** and the **immune system**.

THE MUSCULOSKELETAL SYSTEM

The musculoskeletal system is made up of the bones that form the skeleton as well as the tendons, **ligaments**, cartilage, and muscles that attach to the bones. Bones in the human skeleton have several purposes. They provide a framework for the body. They protect soft organs, such as the lungs and the brain. They also store minerals and produce red blood cells. Most important, the bones provide support that gives the body the ability to move.

A human baby is born with more than three hundred bones in his or her body. As a child grows, some of these bones fuse together. By adulthood, a human has 206 bones. Every bone (except one—the hyoid bone found in the neck) is connected to another bone by a joint.

WHAT IS A JOINT?

A joint is a place where two or more bones meet. The purpose of a joint is to allow repeated and efficient movement. The bones in a joint must be flexible enough to move, but they must also stay in place so that they do not damage each other or come out of the joint. Ligaments keep the bones strapped together. When a joint moves, the ligaments stretch to keep the bones inside the joint. But ligaments only stretch one way, like a rubber band, so that once the movement ends, the ligament returns to its original length and brings the joint back in line.

Some ligaments hold the bones together tightly to prevent the joint from moving the wrong way. For example, an elbow joint will only open and close or move side to side; it will not move backward.

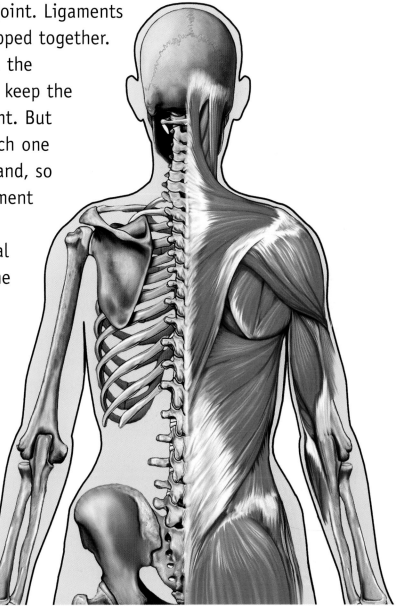

This illustration shows the primary skeletal and muscular anatomy of the female back. Ligaments keep bones together and tendons connect joints to muscles.

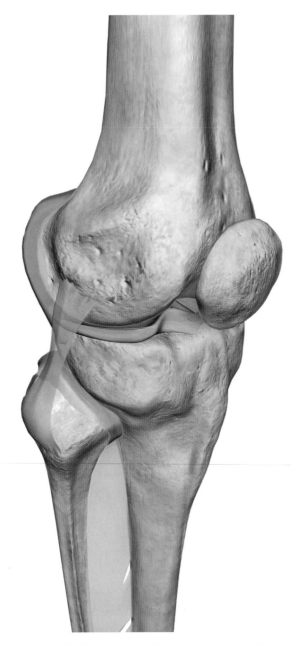

The bones in the knee joint are held together by ligaments (in blue).

Tendons connect bones in the joint to muscles. They are slippery, but they do not stretch. When a muscle receives a message from the brain to move or to rest, the muscle pulls on the tendon and the tendon pulls the joint.

Smooth and spongelike, cartilage covers the ends of the bones in a joint and gives the bones protection from wear and tear. It also provides a cushion to absorb shock. Imagine a basketball player dunking the ball and coming back down to the court. The weight of the player's body could put enormous pressure on the knee joints. This shock would cause unbearable pain if the cartilage in the joint did not soften the blow.

Bones, cartilage, tendons, and ligaments are all made of

connective tissue. Strong and sticky, connective tissue is one of four types of tissue found in the body. It is usually made up of fibers as well as cells that keep the strands knitted together.

In a human **embryo**, most of the bones that form in the first five months are made of cartilage. Later, most cartilage hardens into bone. Other areas do remain as cartilage, such as parts of the nose, outer ear, rib cage, and trachea (windpipe). Cartilage also covers the bones inside joints with a smooth, slippery surface, allowing them to glide against each other easily. Unlike other connective tissue, cartilage does not contain blood vessels. Without the benefit of nutrients found in blood, damaged cartilage is very slow to heal.

Joints are covered in a capsule called a **synovial capsule.** This is a thin membrane that surrounds the joint and creates a joint space. The lining of the capsule releases a thick fluid called **synovial fluid,** which fills the joint space. Synovial fluid works with the cartilage to keep the area between the bones moving smoothly. It also gives nourishment to the cartilage and helps absorb shock.

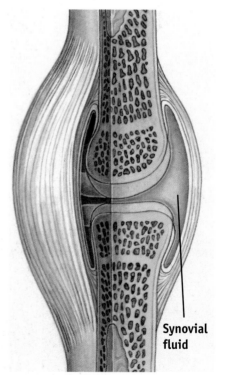

Synovial fluid

This illustration shows a joint with the cushioning of the synovial fluid.

Types of Joints

Type of Joint	Description	Examples
ball and socket	The most mobile type of joint. Ball and socket joints turn forward, backward, and sideways. They can also rotate.	hip, shoulder
pivot	Allows limited side-to-side movement. One bone in a pivot joint is shaped like a ring, and the other is shaped like a cylinder. In some pivot joints, the ring turns inside the cylinder. In others, the ring turns around the cylinder.	neck, forearm

The radius and ulna are the long bones in the forearm. They are joined by pivot joints near the wrist and elbow.

Type of Joint	Description	Examples
ellipsoidal	Allows bending and extending but very little rotating. It is similar to a ball and socket, but the joint is long rather than round.	joint at base of fingers, wrist
gliding	These joints are found between two flat bones that cross over each other.	some joints in wrist and ankle
hinge	Joints that bend in one direction, similar to a hinge that opens and closes a door.	knee, knuckle, elbow
saddle	Rocks side to side and back and forth.	base of the thumb

In some parts of the body, such as in the shoulder or the knee, a few clustered joints are in danger of rubbing against each other. To help smooth the way for tendons that must move across other tendons or bony areas, there are additional sacs containing synovial fluid on the outside of the joints. These sacs are called **bursae**.

WHAT IS OSTEOARTHRITIS?

Osteoarthritis is the most common type of arthritis in the United States. Nearly 27 million Americans have a form of the disease. Though it can strike any joint, the most common joints affected are the hip, knee, lower back, neck, and fingers. Osteoarthritis can affect just one joint or several at the same time.

Osteoarthritis happens when the cartilage coating a bone begins to break down. As the cartilage cracks and wears away, it becomes less able to absorb synovial fluid. This makes the space between the bones narrower and the joint less able to absorb shock. Bones start to rub against each other, and they become pitted and weak. When the bones try to heal themselves, they grow outward and form painful bumps called **osteophytes**, also called bone spurs. Sometimes jagged bits of cartilage break off and float in the joint space. As they float, they scrape away at the bone and the inner lining of the joint capsule.

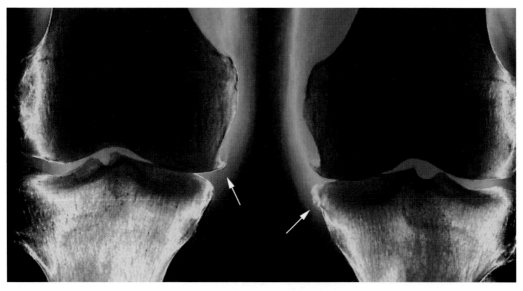

An X-ray of the knees shows an early stage of osteoarthritis, with bone spurs shown in orange.

When the lining of the synovial capsule becomes irritated, it releases enzymes. Enzymes are proteins that set off chemical reactions in the body. These enzymes trigger inflammation and collect in the joint. As the enzymes eat away at the cartilage, the condition gets worse.

THE IMMUNE SYSTEM

The immune system is made up of white blood cells, or **leukocytes**, which travel in lymph vessels and tend to live in organs such as the spleen, thymus, and lymph glands. White blood cells work to fend off **antigens**—germs, bacteria, viruses, and other harmful substances that enter the body.

There are several types of white blood cells. Three types play an important role in understanding rheumatoid arthritis: **phagocytes**, B-**lymphocytes** (known as B-cells), and T-lymphocytes (known as T-cells). When antigens enter the body, certain T-cells, known as helper T-cells, detect the invaders. Helper T-cells alert the B-cells to make a protein called an **antibody**. Antibodies attach themselves to the antigens and form pairs. The pairs travel to the spleen, where the antibody and the antigen are separated. The spleen eliminates the antigens from the body and returns many of the antibodies to the bloodstream for reuse.

Another type of T-cell, called a killer T-cell, attacks the antigen directly with toxic chemicals instead of waiting for B-cells to get involved. Both B-cells and T-cells have the remarkable ability to remember the antigen they have fought. With these memory cells, the immune system can fight off a repeat attacker more quickly.

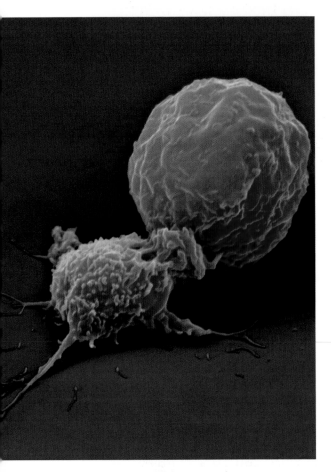

A killer T-cell (in yellow) prepares to destroy a cancer cell (antigen).

The third type of white blood cell needed for a healthy immune system is the phagocyte. *Phagocyte* means "eating cell" in Greek. Phagocytes surround antigens and ingest them.

At a normal infection site, white blood cells gather to attack the antigens. B-cells release tens of thousands of antibodies every second, and the area fills with fluid. This causes inflammation, and it helps weaken the infection and wash away the antigens.

During an infection, white blood cells also produce chemicals that tell the body to send more blood. The added blood flow raises the temperature of the infected area and causes stiffness, redness, and pain. This process is part of the immune system's way of attacking antigens and creating a disagreeable environment for them. It is a healthy immune response.

RHEUMATOID ARTHRITIS

People with rheumatoid arthritis have trouble with their immune system. Their disease falls into a group of diseases called **autoimmune diseases**. In an autoimmune disease, the immune system attacks the body's own healthy tissues as if they are foreign substances.

More than 1.5 million people in the United States have rheumatoid arthritis. The word *rheumatoid* comes from Greek words meaning "similar to a flowing ache." There are many forms of the disease—and many different treatments—but all forms are chronic, and they have no known cure.

Unlike osteoarthritis, rheumatoid arthritis generally strikes people before the age of forty. Scientists do not know why, but in people with rheumatoid arthritis, the body's immune system—its T-cells, B-cells, and phagocytes—act as if the tissues in the joint are antigens. They respond to these false antigens just as they would respond to a true foreign substance.

Rheumatoid arthritis attacks the synovial fluid. A normal synovial membrane is thin, and it produces a thick fluid to bathe the joint. Inflammation makes the synovial membrane

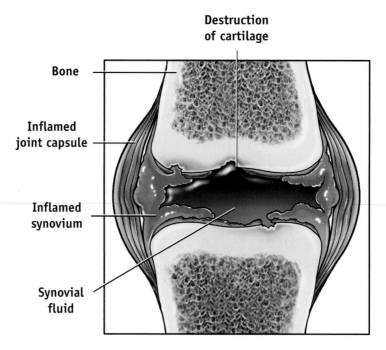

Enlarged view of a joint

This illustration of rheumatoid arthritis shows the destruction of cartilage and bone, as well as inflamed joint capsules.

thick, and its fluid is thin and watery. The thinner synovial fluid does not protect joints from damage, nor does it cushion joints from shock. Without protection, bones knock against each other. Cartilage breaks down, and the ends of the bones wear away. Bones can fall out of the joint or become deformed, and tendons and ligaments can tear. The more damage the joint suffers, the more inflammation occurs, and the painful cycle continues.

Rheumatoid arthritis can affect the whole body, even the spine. Most often it affects fingers, hands, and wrists. Joints on both sides of the body are usually affected at the same time, and sometimes the entire body feels tired and sore. In very severe cases, damage can occur in body parts other than joints, such as the eyes, muscles, skin, heart, and lungs.

JUVENILE RHEUMATOID ARTHRITIS

Juvenile rheumatoid arthritis, or JRA, usually begins between the ages of six months to sixteen years. It is different from adult rheumatoid arthritis. JRA can slow down or speed up the growth of bones. Bones might develop unevenly—for example, one leg may grow longer than the other, or one knee joint may bulge. The most important difference between rheumatoid arthritis and JRA is that some young people affected with JRA can outgrow it. Adult rheumatoid arthritis is a lifelong disease. There are three main types of JRA: polyarticular (Daniel's type

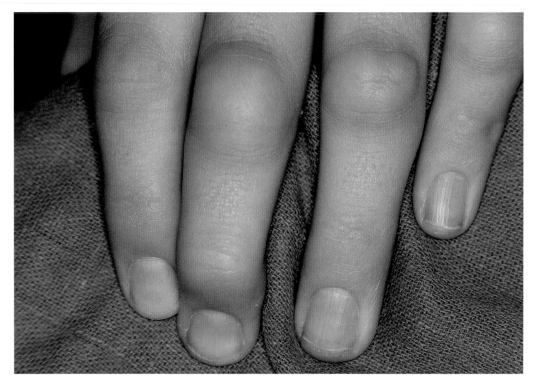

This photo shows rheumatoid nodules on the fingers of a teen that has juvenile rheumatoid arthritis.

from Chapter 1), **pauciarticular**, and **systemic**. Polyarticular JRA affects more than five joints; pauciarticular JRA affects four or fewer joints; and systemic JRA involves the whole body, including the eyes and internal organs as well as joints.

Pauciarticular JRA usually affects large joints such as the knees or elbows. It often affects a joint on just one side of the body. Eyes can become inflamed as well.

Polyarticular JRA affects many joints—mainly the hands and

fingers, but also the knees, hips, ankles, or neck. Usually the same joints on both sides of the body become inflamed. When pain flares up, it often comes with a fever. Bony, misshapen bumps can appear at joints that feel a lot of pressure—for example, from wearing shoes or from sitting on a hard chair.

People with systemic JRA sometimes have high fevers once or twice a day. They may develop a pinkish rash. Joint pain often comes and goes with the fever spikes. The lining around the lungs and heart as well as the lymph nodes and the spleen can become inflamed.

DIAGNOSING ARTHRITIS

Just as there are numerous forms of arthritis, there are many tests that help doctors diagnose the disease. It is important to find out early if a person has arthritis. The sooner patients receive the right kind of treatment, the better chance they have of feeling healthier and preventing further damage to their joints.

Doctors begin with a physical examination. They look for swollen joints, inflammation, rash, fever, or knobby bones. Sometimes none of these symptoms are obvious. In this case doctors might order additional tests, such as X-rays, **magnetic resonance imaging (MRI) tests**, blood tests, or other lab tests. An X-ray can show damage to bones, but it cannot provide information about soft tissue such as muscles or synovial

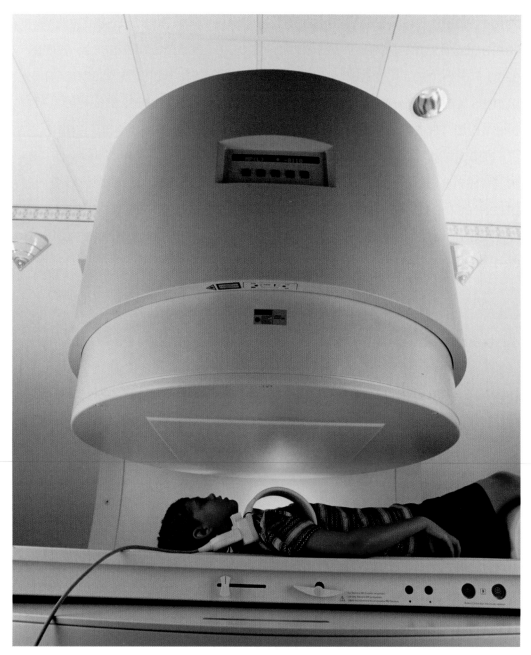

A child undergoes an MRI test in order to find out if he has arthritis.

membranes. An MRI test scans the body using a machine that works with radio waves and magnets. Doctors can look for signs of arthritis in joints and connective tissues.

Doctors can also test the synovial fluid by inserting a clean, hollow needle into a swollen joint and removing a small amount of the fluid. Normal synovial fluid is clear and thick; unhealthy fluid can be bloody, cloudy, and watery. There are also several blood tests that can detect arthritis. Some look for genetic markers showing that the patient has a family tendency toward arthritis. One test, called the Rose-Waaler test, checks for a certain antibody often found in people with arthritis. The antibody is called rheumatoid factor, or RF. Other blood tests measure the level of inflammation in the body.

Most forms of arthritis require specific treatment, so doctors must be very thorough when they diagnose the disease. With a careful examination and tests, health care providers can design treatment plans that are just right for their patients.

3

THE HISTORY OF ARTHRITIS

Arthritis can be traced back to ancient times in both humans and animals. There are signs that some dinosaurs suffered from arthritis, though most experts say that the arthritis found in dinosaur bones was mostly due to joint injuries. A group of iguanodons, unearthed in Europe and dating from 75,000 BCE, had signs of osteoarthritis in their ankles.

The earliest evidence of rheumatoid arthritis was found in the skeletons of people living around 4500 BCE in what is today the southern United States. About two thousand years ago, an Indian medical scholar named Charaka wrote about a disease whose victims had fevers and swollen, painful joints. In 1591, a French doctor named Guillaume de Baillou wrote the first book about arthritis. He called the disease rheumatism and described it by saying, "The whole body hurts, in some the face is flushed; pain is most severe around the joints, so that the slightest movement of the foot, hand, or finger causes a cry of pain"

In the 1600s and 1700s, doctors treated arthritis with medicines made from plants such as Peruvian bark, which contains quinine, and willow bark, which contains the chemical salicylate. Today, modern versions of these medicines are still used to treat arthritis.

In 1859, a British doctor named Sir Alfred Garrod wrote about the disease and gave it the name rheumatoid arthritis. In 1893, Sir William Arbuthnot Lane, a Scottish surgeon working in London, developed a procedure using steel screws and plates to

Elm bark, shown here, helps relieve the inflammation associated with arthritis.

An Arthritis Pioneer:
The Story of Percy Julian

Percy Julian was born in Montgomery, Alabama, in 1899. He was the grandson of a slave. Strict segregation laws were in place, and there were very few public schools that admitted African Americans. Competition was stiff to attend black-only high schools, but Julian was an exceptional student and graduated with honors from the State Normal School for Negroes in Montgomery.

The young man impressed his teachers, and with their help he was accepted into DePauw University in Indiana. Julian studied chemistry and graduated at the head of his class. He went on to study at the University of Vienna in Austria, where he could work without the pressure of the racial prejudice that existed in the United States. In 1931, Julian earned his PhD and became the third African American to earn a graduate degree in organic chemistry.

Dr. Julian returned to the United States with the intention of doing research in medical science at a university. But because he was African American, he was not hired. Instead, he found work at a paint company. Julian continued to do research, especially with plants. He discovered many new compounds, such as a medicine that healed a serious eye disease called glaucoma and a method to use soybeans to make firefighting foam. One of his most famous and important inventions was a synthetic version of the hormone cortisone from an inexpensive wild potato plant from Guatemala. Julian's discovery gave millions of people around the world relief from the pain and suffering of inflammatory diseases, particularly arthritis.

repair bone joints. Hip joint replacement operations became easier after Wilhelm Roentgen discovered X-rays in 1895.

Surgery was rarely used to relieve the pain of arthritis, however. Most medical researchers looked for ways to reduce the pain with medicines. In 1897, a man named Felix Hoffman was working for the Bayer Company, which at the time made dyes for cloth. Hoffman's father suffered from arthritis. With his knowledge of dyes made from plant sources, Hoffman began researching how the salicylate in willow bark eased the pain of arthritis. He discovered a way to mix salicylate with other chemicals to create the painkiller aspirin. Bayer went on to manufacture and sell aspirin around the world. At the same time, doctors who treated their malaria patients with quinine derived from Peruvian bark discovered it could also be used to reduce inflammation in arthritis patients.

The first person to describe how the immune system attacks the body's own healthy joints and tissues was an Australian doctor named Sir MacFarlane Burnet. In 1941, Burnet announced that rheumatoid arthritis is its own disease, apart from osteo-arthritis. In 1948, doctors from the Mayo Clinic in Minnesota injected newly discovered **steroid** hormones into patients with rheumatoid arthritis. This gave patients a great deal of pain relief. Everyone called it a miracle cure—but it did not prove to be a real cure. Now we know that steroid drugs such as **prednisone** have many unwanted side effects, such as weight gain, sleeplessness, and eye problems. However, Burnet's research led to a wide range of drugs that fight inflammation. With the hope of more advances in research, the American Arthritis Foundation was formed in 1948.

MEDICAL ADVANCES TODAY

Experts researching arthritis are looking for the best methods to reduce pain and to help patients function well in daily life. They are studying an important group of drugs called **corticosteroids**, or steroids for short. In laboratories, steroids are made to

MacFarlane Burnet discovered that rheumatoid arthritis was a separate disease from osteoarthritis.

mimic the naturally occurring hormones cortisone and cortisol. These hormones regulate salt and water balance in the body and affect the immune system by reducing inflammation. Corticosteroids in low doses are very helpful in easing pain and inflammation, and in higher doses they are used to attack severe flare-ups. However, using steroids over a long period of time can cause many unwanted side effects and can make the body less able to resist infection.

Although steroid drugs ease the pain of arthritis, many doctors and patients try to avoid them if possible. For many years, scientists have been developing medicines that lessen or prevent inflammation and pain without using steroids. They are called **nonsteroidal anti-inflammatory drugs**, or **NSAIDs**. Some examples of NSAIDs are aspirin, ibuprofen (Advil, Motrin), and naproxen (Aleve). Frequent use of these older NSAIDs can damage the stomach, intestines, and kidneys, however. Researchers continue to look for new NSAIDs that work against inflammation, such as a group of drugs called COX-2 inhibitors. Yet these drugs can also cause problems and side effects.

New NSAIDs go through numerous experiments and clinical trials before they are approved by the Food and

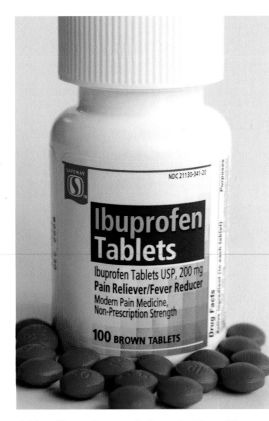

Taking ibuprofen can help arthritis sufferers by reducing inflammation without the side-effects that steroids cause.

Drug Administration (FDA)—the government agency that oversees drug manufacture, research, and licensing. Despite all the caution, every so often patients have severe and unwanted reactions to new arthritis medications. Sometimes, even though the medications were approved, the FDA decides to discontinue them. This is why it is important for researchers to continue developing new pain medications.

Rheumatoid arthritis is a more serious disease than osteoarthritis. To prevent bone damage and abnormal bone growth, researchers look for ways to slow the course of rheumatoid arthritis. Many scientists perform experiments with drugs that work on the immune system. One successful type of drug is called a **disease-modifying anti-rheumatic drug (DMARD)**. Many patients with JRA take a DMARD, such as methotrexate. DMARDS reduce pain and decrease swelling by blocking particular enzymes in the immune system.

Another new type of drug is called a **biologic drug**. Biologics, such as Humira and Enbrel, are medications made from living cells in a laboratory. These powerful drugs block certain proteins that cause inflammation. Scientists have also been investigating certain genes that appear in some people with rheumatoid arthritis. They hope to change this gene to prevent rheumatoid arthritis from developing. Although scientists have not yet found a cure, they have created new combinations of drugs, diets, and therapies that help people with arthritis live stronger, healthier, and less painful lives.

Famous Cases

....

Many famous people have lived with arthritis. Lucille Ball, a talented actress and comedienne, began her career as a model. She suddenly was struck with a fever and learned that she had JRA. Due to her disease, one leg eventually became shorter than the other. She stopped modeling but went on to become one of the best-loved and best-known actresses in the world. Here are a few other famous people who have struggled with arthritis:

Septimius Severus—ruler of the Roman Empire
Bart Conner—two-time Olympic gold medalist in gymnastics
Pierre-Auguste Renoir—French artist
Dr. Christiaan Barnard—heart transplant specialist
Theodore Roosevelt—twenty-sixth president of the United States
George H. W. Bush—forty-first president of the United States

Actress Lucille Ball suffered from juvenile rheumatoid arthritis but went on to become a famous television star and comedienne.

4

LIVING WITH ARTHRITIS

Arthritis affects people in many different ways, so each person must follow his or her own path in living and coping with the disease. Physical therapy, diet, exercise, and medical treatments all play a role in helping patients live as healthy, normal lives as possible.

Sometimes the most difficult part of the treatment process is the diagnosis. There is no one simple test. Rather, doctors perform many tests, such as taking a medical history of the patient, giving a complete physical examination, performing X-rays and other scans such as bone scans, CAT scans, and MRIs. Each of these tests takes a picture of the joints inside of the body. In some instances, doctors will test the blood for signs of infection and inflammation or for a certain gene called a rheumatoid factor (RF) which appears in many, though not all, patients with rheumatoid arthritis. Despite all the available

Exercise, such as yoga, can help those who suffer from arthritis

tools, it is especially difficult for doctors to conclude that a young patient has arthritis. Often, when a young person complains of aches and pains, parents and doctors dismiss the symptoms as growing pains. Once a person is diagnosed with arthritis, however, health care providers should promptly put together a treatment plan.

Arthritis treatment varies with the type and severity of the disease. Most people—especially young people—who follow their treatment plans can look forward to healthier and more active lives. Health care providers should work with patients and their families to form a team. The team usually includes family doctors and specialists such as rheumatologists, orthopedists (doctors who specialize in bone disease), nurses, physical therapists, occupational therapists, nutritionists, podiatrists (foot doctors), ophthalmologists (eye doctors), psychologists, and social workers.

For a patient with mild arthritis, doctors may begin with a treatment plan that includes medications such as NSAIDs or DMARDs to reduce inflammation and to help prevent further joint damage. People with more severe arthritis may be prescribed stronger drugs, such as biologics, or some form of steroid treatment. Analgesics, or painkillers, such as aspirin or ibuprofen can help treat pain, but they should not be combined with some of the other medications. Patients must follow instructions from their doctors and pharmacists.

Physical therapy is an important part of a treatment plan for arthritis. Therapists show their patients how to do a range of motion exercises. These exercises involve slowly opening and closing the joints to their full ability. People with arthritis should do their range of motion exercises twice a day to keep joints flexible, to reduce stiffness, and to help normal bone joint growth. Exercise is also extremely important for people with arthritis. Physical activity helps lubricate the joints and

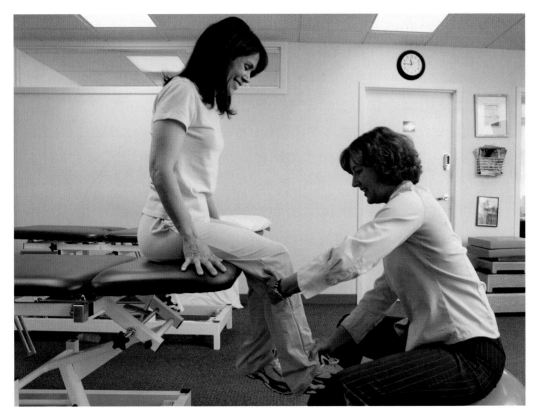

A physical therapist helps a patient with arthritis relieve some of the pain in her joints.

strengthen muscles, which takes stress off joints. Besides reducing pain and increasing joint flexibility, regular exercise gives people more energy and a better sense of well-being. Most treatment plans prescribe a balance of exercise and rest.

Diet is another important part of the treatment plan. People with arthritis have much to gain by eating a balanced diet. Diets rich in whole grains, vegetables, and fruits can help patients maintain a healthy weight. Extra weight puts unnecessary stress on weight-bearing joints such as wrists, knees, hips, and ankles. On the other hand, many people with rheumatoid arthritis experience weight loss. Many of their medicines deprive their bodies of essential nutrients such as vitamins, minerals, and certain proteins. Without these nutrients, patients can suffer from increased inflammation, pain, and intestinal upset. Very often, they must add supplements to their diet. A nutritionist can design diets for people with special needs.

Other important specialists are occupational therapists, ophthalmologists, podiatrists, and orthopedic surgeons. Occupational therapists help people with their small motor skills, such as using a pencil, opening a door, or typing on a keyboard. Arthritis often affects wrists, hands, and fingers. Occupational therapists can provide exercises and assistive devices to ease the symptoms of arthritis. Some assistive devices help people grasp objects. For example, special hooks help people button clothing. Specially shaped pens, scissors, toothbrushes, combs, and silverware are

Eating a diet full of fruits and vegetables will help people with arthritis maintain a healthy weight.

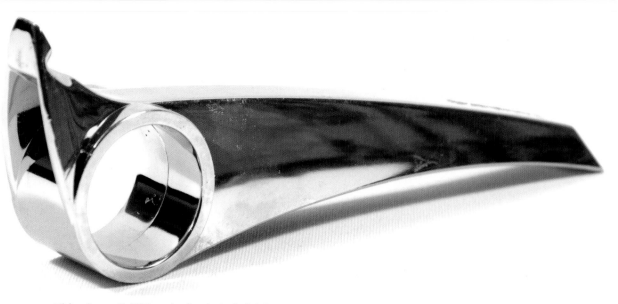

This ringpull lifting devise is helpful for people with arthritis that disables their hands.

available, as well as easy-to-grip foam handles that can be slid onto tools, bicycle handlebars, pots, and pans.

Podiatrists can help people with arthritis ease the stress and pain of affected toe, foot, and ankle joints. Podiatrists sometimes prescribe special supportive footwear or splints, which are molded plastic braces that help keep joints from moving out of line.

Many young people with juvenile arthritis also are at risk for a serious eye condition known as iritis, which is an inflammation of the blood vessels just behind the whites of the eyes. Ophthalmologists use special tests to screen for the condition and provide treatment. Usually eye drops containing steroids control the inflammation.

Young people with rheumatoid arthritis rarely undergo surgery to treat joint damage. But some children with other forms of juvenile arthritis may require surgery if their joints have become too out of line or are deformed. Adults with advanced arthritis, however, often benefit from joint surgery or joint replacement. An orthopedic surgeon oversees this form of treatment.

Everyone with arthritis, no matter what type, experiences pain. Pain management is an essential part of a patient's treatment plan. Pain varies from day to day. Those with mild forms of the disease may take an over-the-counter NSAID such as ibuprofen, while others with more serious forms of the disease may take a combination of prescription drugs. Unfortunately, none of these medicines completely takes the pain away. People with arthritis find other ways of dealing with pain from day to day. Exercise, sports, hobbies, and a positive attitude all help to reduce stress and to help the body "overlook" some of the pain. Some patients successfully use alternative therapies, such as acupuncture, massage, and yoga, along with their medicines. But patients must be sure to give their care providers the details of their treatment plans so that there are no conflicts. Arthritis patients should also be wary of people and websites that try to sell cures. They should absolutely never use a product without consulting members of their treatment team.

Practical Ways to Manage Pain

Everyone with arthritis has periods of time when the pain will not go away and his or her medicine does not help. Sometimes it is hard not to focus on the pain, and at those times, the best thing to do is to think positively and to do whatever it takes to ignore the ache. Scientists have discovered that the body makes proteins and other chemicals (such as endorphins, serotonin, and norepinephrine) that block pain signals sent by nerves to the brain. When people with arthritis encourage their bodies to make extra amounts of these natural painkillers, many find welcome relief from pain. Below are some suggestions.

Distraction techniques:
- pursue a hobby
- call a good friend
- read a funny book or watch an amusing movie or TV show

Relaxing and listening to music you enjoy can help with managing the pain of arthritis.

Relaxation techniques:
- slow, deep breathing
- slowly tighten and relax one muscle group at a time
- relax and listen to soothing music in a calm, quiet space of your own
- sleep on a comfortable mattress and pillow
- use a cold compress (a bag of frozen vegetables or a chilled gel pack) on inflamed joints
- take a warm bath in the morning to soothe aching joints and to relieve tense muscles

Strength-building and endorphin-producing techniques:
- bicycling (use a bike with upright handle-bars and a wide seat or a recumbent cycle)
- weight training
- swimming or warm-water exercises
- yoga or tai chi

Lifting weights helps build strong bones and muscles.

A young boy with arthritis gets a massage as part of a pain management plan.

EDUCATION

Having information about arthritis is the key to coping with the disease. People with arthritis, as well as their friends and families, should learn as much as they can. They should also communicate with their health care team about how the treatment plan is working. When patients are old enough, they should be responsible for taking their own medications and following through with physical therapy.

Patients should definitely speak out when something does not seem right. Local and national organizations offer information about new research, drugs and therapies, clinical trials, coping skills, assistive aids, and more. Libraries, bookstores, and arthritis websites can all offer valuable information. Online social networking websites have arthritis support groups for people of all ages. In these groups, patients can talk to their peers about strategies they use in dealing with school, friends, and coworkers. Newly diagnosed patients can find supportive friends who can share their own experiences with arthritis.

One teen, Jason, says that he does not know anyone else who has JRA. He says it is up to him to teach his friends about his disease so that they are comfortable with him and know what to expect. Some days, he says, he can play soccer or ride a bike with them. But on other days, when his arthritis flares up, he has to take it easy. His friends understand. Jason says, "My friends usually just come over and hang out with me. My thumbs are no good at video games, but we watch movies and just chill. It really helps. They are good guys."

Now that Jason is in middle school, he has a 504 plan. The Rehabilitation Act, a law passed in 1973, grants equal opportunities to Americans with disabilities. Section 504 of that law allows extra accommodations for children with health needs, such as those with arthritis. Once a year, Jason and his parents, teachers, school therapists, and school nurse have a

A Pain Diary

....

During a doctor visit, it can be hard for people with arthritis to recall exactly how much pain they felt, when they felt it, and which joints were the most affected. Often, health care providers encourage their patients to keep a pain diary. Keeping a diary of pain on a daily basis helps caregivers prescribe medicine or suggest ways to improve health and activity levels.

Here are some things to include in a pain diary:

- List every place it hurts.
- Does the pain hurt differently in different places?
- How does it hurt? (ways to describe pain: burning, stabbing, sharp, aching, throbbing, tingling, dull, pounding, pressing)
- Does it hurt more in the morning? Does it change during the day?
- What makes the pain worse? Better?
- Do medicines help? If so, what are the medicines?
- Does the pain cause trouble with eating, sleeping, or daily activities? If so, how?
- What strategies for easing the pain work best (e.g., resting, yoga, distraction, stretching, cold packs, hot bath, massage)?
- What kinds of activities add to the pain (e.g., walking, climbing stairs, typing, bending)?

Having a tutor help with at-home studies is helpful for young patients who may have to miss school when their arthritis flares up.

meeting to decide what extra help Jason may need in school. Some of the items in the 504 plan include having an extra set of books at home, so that Jason doesn't have to carry heavy books back and forth. If he is in a lot of pain, he is allowed to sit out gym class. Jason's plan provides for a home tutor when his JRA flares up and he has to stay home. His teachers e-mail his assignments and excuse him from some of the schoolwork. Some people with arthritis use wheelchairs or canes to get around. For them, and for people such as Jason, whose knee pain can flare up terribly, a 504 plan can allow for the use of an elevator or give students more time to get around between classes.

Jason believes he will get through school just fine. His body is tolerating his medicine, he has good friends, and he has learned to deal with pain flare-ups by taking hot baths, swimming, or just relaxing and listening to music. All in all, he lives his life to the fullest. He hopes to be free of JRA one day, but he knows that many people live with arthritis throughout their entire lives. He is prepared to take care of his health, to stay as active as he can, and to follow the advice of the Arthritis Foundation: "Always focus on what you can do, not on what you cannot do."

GLOSSARY

antibody—A protein, made by the immune system, that fights off germs and other foreign substances.

antigens—Foreign substances, such as bacteria and viruses, that stimulate the immune system to defend itself.

autoimmune diseases—Conditions that cause a person's immune system to attack his or her own healthy cells.

biologic drug—A powerful drug that fights autoimmune diseases such as rheumatoid arthritis.

bursae—Small sacs that are filled with synovial fluid and that sit near the outside of a joint, allowing other bones and tendons to glide over the joint.

cartilage—Connective tissue that covers and cushions the ends of bones in a joint.

chronic—Ongoing; never completely going away.

connective tissue—Tissue that supports and connects the body's cells.

corticosteroids—Natural and synthetic (man-made) hormones that balance salt and water in the body and fight inflammation.

diagnosis—The process of determining the nature of a disease.

disease-modifying anti-rheumatic drug (DMARD)—A type of medication used to decrease pain and inflammation, to reduce or prevent joint damage, and to preserve the structure and function of the joints in people with rheumatoid arthritis.

embryo—The young of a mammal in the early stages of growth in the womb.

immune system—The group of organs, cells, and tissues that recognize foreign substances and defend the body against infection.

inflammation—Swelling, redness, warmth, and pain that happen as a result of trauma, injury, irritation, or infection.

juvenile rheumatoid arthritis (JRA)—An autoimmune disease of childhood in which the body attacks the synovial fluid, tissues, and bones of the joints.

leukocytes—White blood cells.

ligaments—Connective tissues that connect bone to bone inside a joint.

lymphocytes—A type of leukocyte.

magnetic resonance imaging (MRI) tests—Tests of a medical technique that uses magnetic fields to create images of parts of the body.

musculoskeletal system—The system of the body that includes muscles, cartilage, soft tissue, and bones.

nonsteroidal anti-inflammatory drugs (NSAIDs)—Nonsteroid drugs that fight pain and inflammation.

obesity—The state of being extremely overweight.

osteoarthritis—The most common form of adult arthritis, characterized by injury or wear and tear on joints.

osteophytes—Bony growths at the ends of bones, also called bone spurs.

pauciarticular—Affecting four or fewer joints.

phagocytes—White blood cells that fight invading cells by ingesting them.

polyarticular—Affecting five or more joints.

prednisone—A synthetic steroid drug.

rheumatologist—A doctor who specializes in diseases of the immune system.

steroid—One of many natural carbon based compounds found in the body. Synthetic steroids are used as a medication to relieve inflammation and swelling.

synovial capsule—The casing around a joint.

synovial fluid—Fluid in the joints and bursae that acts as a lubricant for joints and tendons.

systemic—Throughout the entire body.

tendons—Fibrous bands of tissue that connect muscle to bone.

FIND OUT MORE

Organizations

Arthritis Foundation
P.O. Box 7669
Atlanta, GA 30357-0669
800-283-7800
www.arthritis.org

Arthritis National Research Foundation
200 Oceangate, Suite 830
Long Beach, CA 90802
800-588-2873
www.curearthritis.com

Centers for Disease Control and Prevention (CDC), National
Center for Chronic Disease Prevention and Health Promotion,
Arthritis Section
Mailstop K-51
4770 Buford Highway NE
Atlanta, GA 30341-3724
770-488-5464
www.cdc.gov/arthritis/index.htm

National Institute of Arthritis and Musculoskeletal and Skin
Diseases (NIAMS)
National Institutes of Health
1 AMS Circle
Bethesda, MD 20892-3675
877-226-4267
www.niams.nih.gov/

Books

Rouba, Kelly. *Juvenile Arthritis: The Ultimate Teen Guide*.
Lanham, MD: Scarecrow Press, 2009.

Scott, Rosanna. *Peter and Friends at Camp*. Hollidaysburg, PA:
Jason and Nordic Publishers, 2006.

Websites

American Academy of Pediatrics—Arthritis
www.aap.org/healthtopics/arthritis.cfm

Kids Health—Juvenile Rheumatoid Arthritis
www.kidshealth.org/kid/health_problems/bone/juv_rheum_
arthritis.html

emedicinehealth—Juvenile Rheumatoid Arthritis
www.emedicinehealth.com/juvenile_rheumatoid_arthritis/
article_em.htm

The National Library of Medicine—Arthritis
www.nlm.nih.gov/medlineplus/arthritis.html

INDEX

Page numbers for illustrations are in **boldface**.

ABOUT THE AUTHOR

Ruth Bjorklund lives on Bainbridge Island, a ferry ride away from Seattle, Washington, with her husband, two children, and five pets. She has written several books about health issues and has a great respect for people who live with arthritis and for people who provide them with care and support.